CW01522030

ELEMENTAL

CENTRAL OTAGO POEMS

ELEMENTAL

CENTRAL OTAGO POEMS

BRIAN TURNER

PHOTOGRAPHS BY GILBERT VAN REENEN

GODWIT

 The assistance of Creative New Zealand is gratefully acknowledged by the publisher.

A GODWIT BOOK published by Random House New Zealand
18 Poland Road, Glenfield, Auckland, New Zealand

For more information about our titles go to www.randomhouse.co.nz

A catalogue record for this book is available from the
National Library of New Zealand

Random House New Zealand is part of the Random House Group
New York   London   Sydney   Auckland   Delhi   Johannesburg

First published 2012

© 2012 text Brian Turner; images Gilbert van Reenen

The moral rights of the author have been asserted

ISBN 978 1 86979 741 6

This book is copyright. Except for the purposes of fair reviewing
no part of this publication may be reproduced or transmitted in
any form or by any means, electronic or mechanical, including
photocopying, recording or any information storage and retrieval
system, without permission in writing from the publisher.

Design: Megan van Staden
Printed in China by Everbest Printing Co Ltd

For those who love and
understand Central Otago,
wherever they live.

———————

CONTENTS

MUSIC IN THE MOUNTAINS

In the sharpest weeks of winter
    Sibelius is the musical choice
of the clouds that jostle
    and slide across a stony-blue sky

and Beethoven's always there, eminent
    on stormy days; and in the evenings,
when skies have cleared, it's quiet
    for the willows by the stream

have stopped conducting for the day.
    Then, in summer, Mozart's
in the creeks jouncing off the hills,
    flickering in the leaves,

Elgar and Mahler and Dvořák are
    sonorous in the mountain valleys
late in the day when we sit
    on verandahs drinking

and eating and yarning while a
    mischievous moon makes cut-out
shapes on the flats and the breeze
    makes music for the stars.

FOREWORD

n my experience, one of the most common questions we ask each other is, 'Where do you come from?' In my case I've never had much trouble answering that because for as long as I can remember I was convinced I came from a marvellous part of not just New Zealand but The World. And a lot of that belief came from the fact that for the most part the countryside, the rivers and streams, the forests, and the seas around our coasts were in fairly good shape, weren't badly out of balance.

I enjoyed hearing my parents and grandparents talking about *the past*, liked hearing their accounts of days before my advent. It goes without saying that we all spend plenty of time yakking about the present. No one I knew well took anything for granted, and most were thankful for small mercies. Ingratitude was frowned upon.

My father's mother only ever crossed Cook Strait, saw Wellington, once in her long lifetime. So in 1968, when I told her that I was off to work there, she said, 'What's wrong with Dunedin?' Not much, in my view, and I still think that.

More and more, and especially since I returned to Otago in 1974, I found myself saying, 'I come from southern New Zealand.' I'd discovered I had an intense desire to draw others' attention to 'our' place, to what was happening here, both good and bad. I felt we had a duty to properly love and care for this land and its waters.

Years later Margaret Atwood was to put it nicely when she said of the world in general, 'without a functioning biosphere (clean air, clean water, clean earth and a variety of plant and animal life) we will starve, shrivel, and choke to death'. As a species we don't seem to have 'got' that yet, or can't work out and agree on what to do about it.

My love of and interest in what goes on in the outdoors came alive in the 1950s, when my parents often took us inland on fishing trips. I greatly liked the tussock-cloaked country near Lake Mahinerangi, about 60 kilometres west of Dunedin. To me that was where my Central Otago began, and to hell with boundaries drawn on maps. I wrote about it in my memoir *Somebodies and Nobodies*:

> *A huge, tawny expanse rolled west. Often there were great bursty clouds in otherwise blue skies. The land and skyscapes were stirring, inspirational, and the phrase 'Where there's a will there's a way' was never far from my mind. This wasn't 'my' country, it was 'ours'. For the first time I realised I belonged here; for the first time I felt a depth of attachment stronger than anything I'd experienced before.*

I've never once lost that feeling, doubted the truth and sincerity of it.

I can now see why I was attracted to and admire the work of writers here and elsewhere who have an intimate association with, understanding of and ability to vividly evoke — in several senses — the places they come from and, or, grow to love. I've long felt, as the American writer Flannery O'Connor — who hailed from the American

South — remarked, that if you wanted to become a writer you'd 'better come from somewhere'.

Another American of great distinction, Bill McKibben, wrote of 'the surpassing glory of our right habitation of a place'. That compelled me to ask to whom and what do we have duties, and what are they? I believe they must include proper stewardship of the natural world, exercising care which is underpinned by an acceptance that life is not 'all about us' but about what's *all* about us. As Aldo Leopold asserted, something is right when it tends 'to preserve the integrity, stability, and beauty of the biotic community' and 'wrong when it tends otherwise'. He also said we desperately needed to adopt a land ethic, see the world around us 'as a community to which we belong' rather than 'a commodity belonging to us'.

I chuckled when I first read Wendell Berry, who said that humans not only 'have problems . . . we are problems'. Which is no doubt why he said, when writing of one dam proposal, that it wasn't 'a definitive solution to any problem, upstream or down. Like many another project that has been offered to the people as a lasting monument of human progress, it is a cheap shortcut.' I wish someone in Central Otago would convince the directors of Pioneer Generation of that.

For decades I've believed, as Robert Macfarlane wrote in *The Guardian*, that 'the fate of nature and the fate of humanity are inseparable', and that as a society we have allowed too much indiscriminate change of a kind that has caused irrevocable damage to our world. Ironically a lot of such activity is still termed — possibly unthinkingly — as 'progress and development'. The result is often a falsification of the reality.

In recent years I've often been called an activist. I see

that as a compliment. Inactivity is not for me. I see little merit in endorsing the intensification of more of the insensitive same. And nor does the columnist and essayist Dave Witherow, who witheringly observed that:

> *Without memory, and without the anger*
> *that memory evokes, we surrender*
> *all that is best of our country to the*
> *complacent, the greedy and the ignorant,*
> *who in due course, will wreck it all,*
> *chirping that they live in Paradise.*

And I also note Sir Alan Mark's poignant reminder that 'Over [his] lifetime [he'd] witnessed continued losses of our unique natural heritage' and that 'Sadly conservation seems mostly involved in reducing the rate of loss.'

What Mark says is undeniable, which is why I tend to encourage NIMBY*ism. If we all looked after our lands and waters properly the whole world would be in far better shape.

Otago's high country valleys have long entranced me. I delight in wandering there when a wind's coquettish in my hair, the sun's warm, and I can listen to the water burbling in streams that are cool, clean and clear.

In my book *Into the Wider World* I wrote of times when:

> *I have lain in long waving grasses, gazed at the*
> *snow-flecked mountains and listened to the larks,*
> *the pipits, the cicadas sing and rasp; watched bees*
> *dithering, heard them buzzing. Watched a hawk*
> *shadow a hare, and the hare bound and hurry to*
> *avoid oblivion.*

---

* Not in my backyard

Poets — certainly poets like me — end up finding and revealing the self in where they come from, and hope to be able to say, eventually, *this is where I most belong*. All writers, not just poets, are explorers, archaeologists too; we grub, we dig, are often surprised by what we find. There is music, there is song, there is grace and, now and again, a place where peace of mind is at home; then one can feel confident and, for magical moments, comfortable and at ease. There, truly, is a wonderful place to be.

On such occasions I sense there's something of the numinous, something sacred, in and about our surroundings. I mean this in a broad-brush spiritual sense. It's as if the hills watch us, and ask if we are watching ourselves in them.

All of which is to argue that words and images and the world of 'nature' itself sometimes take on an ardent life of their own; they are intent on seduction, and who would want to resist. I hope my poems at times take readers to places they've not been before, and that they have fidelity to what can be found and experienced there.

Brian Turner
Ida Valley
March 2012

PART ONE

EARTH

WHAT IT'S LIKE

When someone asks you to explain
what it's like where you come from
you say you're still finding out,
and it's not because you enjoy being
vague, or smart-arse, a sophist
if you like, it's just because it's true.

This morning frost then fog like smoke
from a damp wood fire, then the sun
breaking through in lamé-like patches
until there's not even bandannas
left on the hills, and order's restored:
blue sky above incandescent snow.

ALP

—

The alp at the end of the street
— Stevens' *Notebooks*

The alp at the end of the street
is known to all
as His Imperious Majesty

moody   radiant   properly aloof
and crowned   sometimes
with heavy-weight cloud

and although he likes to wear
a robe
of royal blue

pomp is not his true style
except when he's enthroned
beneath brilliant stars

on summer nights
reflecting the edgy light
of the moon

that rolls above him
a royally minted gold coin
and each generation of townsfolk knows

that whenever
grandeur's required
it's over to him

ROCK AND PILLAR

There's a big grubby underbelly
    to the coverlet of cloud
spilling off the Rock and Pillar
    and a singer whose name escapes me
is certain *we are nowhere*
    and it's now. I have to say No,
but I know what I think he means.

A fresh sharp westerly is bulked
    by the chill of snow. The sun
blares. The roadside grasses
    shiver. Tufts of sheep pick
at bare paddocks. Everywhere rock
    outcrops lie about like litter
that can't be removed though some
    have tried to tidy the place
up a bit to make it feel less like
    nowhere you'd like to be
and more like the somewhere it is.

BIKING THE CENTRAL OTAGO RAIL TRAIL

From Waipiata, north to Wedderburn
on a clear, still, bright autumn Saturday,

it's airy and eerie on the old rail trail,
the land sloping right to left

from the Ida and Hawkdun ranges
to the Taieri headwaters, the ridgelines

cut into the sky, the mountains hanging
as if suspended in air rather than

rising out of the brown-top land.
The day's tricked up but not tricked out

and the line runs straight on to Ranfurly
and out the other side, going west.

POOLBURN TWILIGHT

Where I come from
the hills are conceived
in the late evening's afterglow
and grow slowly
through the night

and they are there
wet and shining
in the wondrous mornings.
I guess you know
there's truth in that,

but unless you are alert
in the half-light
before dark
and follow the contours
east west north and south,

mapping the land,
how are you to know
which are newly-born
and which
were there before?

THROUGH

You give out and you take back
and, gradually, you're absorbed
into the land that absorbs you.
Imperceptible's the word that divines
the movement of shadows
extending or withdrawing
from the gulleys where tussocks
congregate and nod assent
when mountain winds
begin to talk. And, all through
whatever happens, whatever evolves,
rock outcrops crane
from the ridgelines
and take what comes.
And what comes, comes together
one way or another,
whatever you do; and wherever
you go, goes with you
until you're through.

VAN MORRISON IN
CENTRAL OTAGO

Take me back to the days
before rock and roll,
Life with Dexter and
the Goons, days when
Dad and Dave still bumbled
in Snake Gully
and the skies were not
cloudy all day, before

I saw tussock, heard it
speaking in tongues
and chanting with the westerly:
What's productive here
is what's in your heart,
sworn through your eyes,
ears, the flitter of the
wind in your hair;

the smell, the taste
of air from the mountains,
off flats where the river
runs from somewhere north
to somewhere south and the sky's
forever. It's not picturesque,
it's essential, almost
grand, and it aches

like the rhythms of truth
scornful of tittle-tattle.
You have to be here, you
have to feel the deep
slow surge of the hills,
the cloak of before, the wrench
of beyond. You know
what, you know

not. And that's what
makes it heart-stopping,
articulate, hurtful
like resuscitation.
You cannot bear to use
the word again again
when driven by an urge
to begin to begin.

TANGATA WHENUA

The station's a yellowy white box
surrounded by tarry gravel
dry grass
and an emptiness that seems to go on
and on

and the railway line's
a silent arrow
buried in a cutting
now that trains
don't run

the huge sky
ekes out the summer twilight
and down by the river
two piebalds are stroked by shadows
from the willows

the country
rolls through me
and stretches away as I lie back
and wait for the first bright stars
to prick the quilted sky

PLACE

———

Once in a while
you may come across a place
where everything
is as close to perfection
as you will ever need.
And striving to be faultless
the air on its knees
holds the trees apart,
yet nothing is categorically
this, or that, and before the dusk
mellows and fails
the light is like honey
on the stems of tussock grass,
and the shadows
are mauve birthmarks
on the hills.

ABANDONED HOMESTEAD

A family lived here   in this homestead
on a terrace   above a wide valley
with a river running down   to a glacial lake

In the distance are mountains   blue and black
and   closer   the river winding
thin and waxy like floss

Dust   droppings   cobwebs   straw
the house is full of signs of uninvited guests
and on a shelf beside the range
I find a piece of wood
inscribed with the words   Agnes Brown toiled here

To my knowledge   there is no other record
of what she thought or said   so we're not
going to know   what she did
when the man she lived with   was riding
the farthest boundaries of the run

And we can only imagine   what she said
to her children   when they left home
headed for the big smoke   one supposes
they drove off   harness jangling   dust
puffing from hoofs and wheels   the cart
rocking and bouncing along the track   but
how long she stood there   after the cart
had gone   we cannot say

The summer evenings are long here
and we assume she sat   on the verandah
knitting or reading   watching the ridges
for the shape of a man on a horse
silhouetted against the flare
from the setting sun

More than a lifetime has passed   and the wood
where I sit   on that same verandah
is rotted now   and the evening light's
like panic   on the cracked windows
behind me   and in the west
the sky is tangerine   and the mountains turning black

LAST OUTING

She waited for him to come home,
knowing where he was
yet wondering just the same.

He was on the hill, among
the grey, lichen-braised rocks,
the creamy, straw-coloured grasses,

in a world where clouds
defer to blue sky, and hawks
are as much languor as threat

in flight. A world where sheep
look at you as if querying
your right to be there, and quail

behaviour is snickery, irascible.
As the sun went down she knew
the far hills reminded him

of all they hadn't done as much
as what they had, in their place,
together, the evening light

that haunts the way home does.

LAWRENCE CEMETERY

(FOR NGAIRE)

―――――――

An artist takes snaps of cemeteries
irresistibly, *click*, with light
angling in from the left, say,
or the right, shadows staining headstones
and neglected plots, rusty iron
fencing off the last small pieces of land
that are definitely not ours.
One walks with care on such impenitent ground.

The sun dazzles and sprags
like a splinter in the corner
of your eye. Late light genuflects
upon the nearby hills: distantly
mountains turn gun-metal blue.
It feels quite neighbourly, you say,
picking a path among the broken vases
and the perky faces of wild flowers.

WEST OVER THE MANIOTOTO

(AFTER SYDNEY)

———————————

The pathos of absence is eloquent here
where who preceded whom matters less
    than where they came from, what
they did, and why; matters less than
    questions like whether it makes
sense to revere place or repeat practice,
and whether superseded is only
another soulless name for disregard.

In fact, few lived here, ever; most
passed through en route to parts
    hardly known. Stone was hewn,
moa slaughtered, grasslands burnt –
    as everywhere else – except it all
took more time and effort then, a different
sort of know-how, but with little evidence
of a hunger for conspicuous wealth. All

in the name of progress, of course. You
could ask if this landscape invites reflection
    or is such purely a function of individual
sensibilities? And could it be that here
    the imagination's married to humility
that's free to roam in realms stripped
of the pomp of narrow perspectives, and foreignness
is what we cannot find within ourselves?

BRACKEN

Where are they now,

the haymakers in the fields
along the road to kingdom come,
the sow with her
tussocky-coloured torpedos
disappearing into tunnels
in a waving sea of bracken,
the woman you were
and the man I was,
beached on our backs
staring at a piece of moon
like a parapente
in realms without name
high above
where clouds don't reach.

LOOKING FOR REAL LIFE
AND THE REAL WORLD

Self-pity's a tumour,
which is why you look to what
the land around you says
in order to feel less like
a nowhere soul. Land

in which the seasons come and go
as clouds do, where rivers flow
above and underground
and the more you look and listen
the more you get to know

about the yearly round's
resemblance to moods
of troubled hearts and minds.
A land where winter's harsh,
scintillating, spring unrestrained,

summer trance-like and blustery
by turns, autumn sober,
austere, and shifting angles of light
give clarity and new perspectives
everywhere you look, from cup-caked

scattered outcrops of rock or
backyards in which are strewn
the relics from days in essence
little different from this, days
when most still wrestled to define

what legions mean by *real life*
in the vexing *real world*
and to understand why it's so
disobedient, out of control, refuses
to be compliant to our every wish.

YELLOW FLOWERS, OTUREHUA

There's a field of rampant, pale yellow flowers
east of the road north of Oture.
Thirty acres of the bloody stuff, the farmer says,
and I'm damned if I know what it's called.
Unobtrusive for months, now it's grown like fury
beneath wide skies where clouds are stalled.

I can't tell him the name either. He says,
with a dismissive sweep of a hand,
the sheep don't like it much, so I guess
it's there to stay. It's roots go deep, which,
given his surname, irks to understand
his attachment here, too. There's a rich

vein of family histories going back
to days when gold was what you took
and then moved on, leaving land to wrack
but not quite ruin. *If you find out*
what it's called let me know, it'll be in a book
somewhere. Anyway, your shout.

He has easily the best-known, most
photographed paddock in the district, and
he knows it. We drink a toast
to flowers, to the good life *as long*
as you don't weaken. He's a man of the land
for whom not much has gone wrong.

I see you've moved in, think you'll stay?
he asks. *Aw yeah, I guess so, until the day . . .*

ENSEMBLE

Around here rampaging in paddocks
and along roadsides are woolly
yellow-flowered green-leaved
mulleins, blue viper's bugloss,
clover and yarrow galore, plants

taller and more prolific than for years
because of a wet December. And
there are hefty rust-red Herefords
and fat lambs and old woollies aplenty
tottering on the rock-dotted, green

and brown-splotched hills. Add
the likes of me becoming, as one kid
put it, a Bifocal Identity, a bloke
called Crocodile, another known as
Dynamite, and words such as

polyglot and conglomerate take on
new meanings. Then there's a man
I'm calling Noah – he's collected one
of just about every bit of old machinery
there is. As for other plants, hillsides

are scented by wild thyme and roses,
roadsides sport daisies and Californian
poppies, and I'd like to think
there's some sweet william tucked away
somewhere; and later, high on the

Old Man Range there'll be gentians
where the fellfields are, where
sunlit schist and scree turn slopes
into shining shields. I'm saying
the world's a symphony, that

there's an ensemble somewhere
wherever we are and we're part of it
though not all have seen it yet
and who knows which names, which
of them and us will linger and last?

PASTORAL

The Spirit responds to names
  lucerne barley wheat
  maize corn rye-grass sorrel

Trust their names
  for as long as you
  speak them

They testify to the powers
  of the sun and the rain
  to what we know

Of the pull of the earth
  face up to that Spirit
  and the earth

To which I am dumb
  and which cannot speak
  the language of fools

APPLE PICKING

Go towards and by the rusting wires,
the twisted waratahs, through thistle

and rye-grass and speckled yarrow,
to the old, scabby apple tree

by the rail trail at Auripo. Pick
the yellow and green-hued apples

flecked in autumn, the few left
like wan globes on branches

whose leaves are wearied. Pick
them to feed to birds in the depths

of winter when their chittering
speaks of gratitude more than

anything else you can easily think of.
Each apple's a blessing, and a gift,

as each day is, be it sloughing autumn
or any other season. Pick, and pick,

then leave with a wry smile
and a longing to be back next year.

APPLICATIONS

The land, touched up
by the startle
of a summer morning,

tones down
in the evenings,
distils us

as we distil it.

ONCE GREEN

As summer insists
   the roadsides are a riot
of blue purple yellow white
   and orange wild flowers,

and over the fence, on stony
   burnt-grassed ground,
sheep, cattle and deer graze
   what's left of grass once green.

MOVING STOCK

A curdle of sheep wobbles by
leaving freckles
and liver spots
all over the road.

OPPORTUNITY KNOCKS

That big bull
in the scruffy paddock
under the hill
bordered by a meek
late summer creek
never bothers anyone
until opportunity knocks
and he decides
it's time he was
in the money
again. He bellows,
mounts. You can
hear him a good
mile away, at least,
and the whole valley
knows about it.

BEASTS

The beast that used to look at me
more unblinkingly
than I can look at others,
and for longer, is dead
and not from natural causes.

He was slaughtered
before he became inedible,
by one who says he loves animals,
in order to supplement his income
and maintain a viable farm.

I'm not going to argue
with a man of the land,
with what is part
of everyday life in the country.
And besides, I'm a meat-eater myself,

but I did like that Hereford's tan,
his mute white patches,
the shine on his hoofs,
the way he scuffed the ground
and the noise, which, when he farted

was like a tube unblocking mud.
I saw us sharing an ability
to splat borne of rumination
without roughage, and a habit
moseying without felonious intent.

Now he's mostly fat, flesh, bone,
the grace and wonder of his structure
dismantled. I'm not going
to moon about it, for others fill
the space he roamed in front

of the Hawkduns, in sun wind
rain and snow. But I won't forget
how good he looked there,
in space I still move in,
and how we shared what others

no longer share. We had
a stake here, that beast and I,
and I still have some say
in what he would not have thought
to take away from me.

FARMER

On a fine day, the sun shining bright,
   the sky a peerless deep blue bowl,
with a warm wind filtering
   through the orchard's trees,
and willows swaying on the banks
   of fast-running streams,
the land seems unalterably kind.

And when the blood's moving freely
   in my veins, the tractor's
throbbing beneath me, and the furrowed
   earth's opening, stretching
out behind, I am happy in what I know.

KEEP IT UP

_____

A farmer asked me
if I was working
and added
he didn't mean
writing.
        I said
I was sawing
and stacking wood,
tidying the shed,
pruning the hedge.
'Is that work?'

'Yes,' he said,
'keep it up.'

DOGS

The dogs on the back
of the battered ute
are up and down
like dominoes
despite the barking
from the one
behind the wheel
who used to play
the national game
with 'a bit of the mongrel
in 'im'. When he stops
they all pile off
and a ruck forms.

RUMINATIONS IN THE MANIOTOTO

The belted galloways with the off-white band
around their middles,
          and their mostly black
everything else, look well-designed and docile

to me. It's easy to approve of them,
and hard for me to think
          of ways they could
have been improved on – and why bother?

Not that I want to get into arguments
about whether or not
          some sort of grand
almighty cosmic architect might have

had a hand in putting them together
in order to have us all
          forever and a day
wail in wonder at His or Her marvellous

handiwork. Knowing that bulls and cows
obey what appears to be
          nature's imperatives
is enough of an explanation for me,

and not worth fighting over. So let those
animals remain belted
                    rather than battered,
heads down and munching grass,

and long unbothered by me as I pass.

MATAKANUI
(FOR MARIE HOPKINS)

When hay's in the fields in November
  and the moon's high in the sky,
these are the days you'll remember
  forever, without a word of a lie.

In the north the Dunstans are browning
  yet few of the streams are dry,
and above us the hawks are turning
  in the unending blue of the sky.

To the south the Raggedies rumple
  and the Old Man Range angles
down, and skylines galore crumple
  on horizons sliding away. Bangles

of light glitter on every pond
  that pied parries ceaselessly
patrol. It's as if we share a bond
  that will never be broken. Sleepily,

as night begins to fall like down,
  and the far hills fade from sight,
the stars above are a heavenly town
  illuminated by magical light.

The nor'wester buffets and blows,
  scents of bugloss and thyme fill the air
and the gold light of evening glows
  at the end of days without peer.

Drybread and Tinkers and Matak
  have an aura of days of yore,
of those who left and never came back
  and live on here only in lore.

But once you've embraced Central
  and fallen in love with the land,
you'll always be, perennial,
  imbued with a love that's grand.

FILMING AT LOWER NEVIS

Here one reflects on what McKibben means
    when he writes of a wish to achieve in time
a 'right habitation of a place' for all our time.
    Needs not wants is where one starts

and maybe ends in a place where stoicism speaks
    and ambition's arrested, where skies
over the hills and mountains dress the valley
    with light and shade more real than chimerical.

Silence, when broken, will not be suppressed,
    the far off seems close at hand
and the wind's hiss in the sparse grass
    is conspiratorial, both a welcome and a warning.

Some lived out their days here but many more
    came and left, taking their impressions with them,
leaving their imprints behind. The early evening's gifts
    include a bright new moon that temporarily

subdues transcience, but there's no sign
    that an Indian summer's under way,
there's just the past's aura in the present
    and across the flats, where oats once grew

and sheep still graze, grey and brown mullocky
    hunches in heaps, while under the hill
the river swings back and forth playing the music
    of melting snow. Complacency never took root here,

and shibboleths were swept away in country
    where little appears to have changed
since the days when the back of beyond
    and the wild blue yonder were everywhere

no more than an hour away, and every campsite's
    ashes were warm, even when abandoned by those
who sought and preferred solitude's solace to pointless
    ease wherever it could be found and kept alive.

HOMECOMING

When I left the leaves were falling fast,
the grass unusually green and long,
yet nothing is pandered to here.
Gravity and land are synonymous,
as is the grace that goes with elegant skies.

When I returned the ground was hard,
the snow crisp and starkly white,
the willows brittle, bare, with a bravery
I don't have. When I lit the woodburner
and the house began to creak, and warmth
spread, I began to feel at home once more.

What's worthwhile takes time. Tomorrow,
I thought, what's fine will become
familiar again, what's familiar, fine.

HILLS

————

Someone said the hills
were slumbering in the heat.
Another said
they were meditating.
My friend said
they were talking crap,
those two, that hills
were there for tussock
and bracken and gentians
to grow on. They all
had an idea about
the hills. I said
we're all hills too
and that they would
watch us with amusement
until we died
at which point there would be
no argument
as to who was
or was not a hill.

HOME HILLS, FEBRUARY
(FOR GRAHAME SYDNEY)

It's said that autumn's already on its way
  by those who know about such things
and yet, truly, few things matter less
    this afternoon, a few miles up the road
from Hills Creek where Baxter spent
  holidays in his youth, dived into the race
and swam through the culvert
    under the road where tree roots
could easily have trapped him.

It must have been 60 years, or more, ago,
  when several houses squatted there
and trees were smaller and fewer,
    and the sod cottage nearest
the main road corner wasn't used – though
  who really knows? – by a foxy 70-year-old
and a younger woman who looks, locals say,
    barely a quarter his age.

Today, there's just me, Jacquie the aged golden lab
  whose coat is like bleached tussock,
and the painter Grahame Sydney. The Hawkduns
    to the north, Home Hills and their easy curves
to the west, and a few fluffy clouds
  primping in the distance above Moa Creek
and the Poolburn's sprawling hills trending south
    at the far end the Ida Valley.

A warm and gentle wind puffs intermittently,
  flies buzz, and, ambling – in my case hobbling,
due to stitches in my abdomen – one needs to
      beware of lancing spaniards, whose
late flower-stems are bowed and tatty
  like the standards of a beaten army.

Syd's spotted the yards, iron woolshed, bunkhouses
  and a three-roomed roughcast cookhouse
whose long wooden table seats at least twelve.
      He says, 'I see several paintings here,'
as he lifts his sketch pad, clip board
  and small red canvas folding stool from his vehicle
and sets out to make some pencil drawings.
      He finds a spot among late dandelion,
purple-headed thistles, stunted matagouri,
  rabbit scrapes, sheep shit, dry grey plonks
of cattle dung, clumps of tussock, and pink
      and white clover gone to seed. Old iron
and rotting timber is clamped in the wavier grass . . .
  so much to comprehend in all
that is past its best and yet not past.

An elderberry girds part of one wall
  of the woolshed – used mainly for crutching
now, and storing saddlery for the hacks
      that graze undisturbed nearby –
and delicate willows sprout from a soak
  30 metres away. Inside the shed
and bunkrooms, walls and floors and wire
      mattresses are streaked with bird-droppings.
Brooms and scrapers are propped against
  holding pens; hooks hang from rafters.

Concrete piping lies against a wall; cupboards
        and safes are missing doors,
windows are broken, gappy as memory.
    Grey and white gulls' feathers flitter
around the base of a drum half full of stretchy tar.

I stroke the muzzle of a chestnut hack
    that sidles up to the fence
behind the woolshed, while the dog,
        belly wet and dirty from digging up
a hedgehog's nest, slobbers and sniffles,
    collapses panting in the shade
of a tussock. Birds chitter and fuss
        but can't suppress the noise
this sprawling country makes.

'I won't be long,' Syd says, 'just one more drawing.'
    For once we are not men behaving sadly
or badly, but gladly. And looking north
        towards the head of the Manuherikia
the farther off the bluer the hills become.

DESERTS, FOR INSTANCE

The loveliest places of all
are those that look as if
there's nothing there
to those still learning to look

REMEMBERING SUMMER

The memory of what you'd love to do again
  is on the rise. You'd run bare foot
over the grass on a summer's evening,

the sky like candy in the west
  where the wind and the sun die down,
watch light flickering in the bounce

of water flowing over a cobbly bed
  of gorgeous yellow, green and brown stones,
your mother's voice calling you home.

CLOSE OF DAY, OTUREHUA

The sun's gone down behind Blackstone Hill
and the nearby pines are still. There's
not a breath in the willows by the Ida,
but we don't need a breeze
to confirm that the world's alive

and full of promise, inspiriting.
Dogs bark and snarl, chains rattle;
my neighbour is calling
for a daft black lab called 'Boy'
to come home *Now*.

The sky is clear as conscience,
tonally pure, and in the paddock
under the hill, cattle are grunting
as if trying to shove mountains aside.

THERE YOU ARE

The only roads one knows well
are grit-spread tracks
that lead back to oneself
and a voice
that won't go away says
There you are
as you are.

JULY, MANIOTOTO

There are mountains
    everywhere
and the snow's trying
    to hide them.

You don't have to
    climb a mountain
to find yourself
    climbing one.

There's always another
    and another, and
to think some fools
    used to say

they went out and
    conquered them.

PART TWO

FIRE

FALLS DAM

For a moment there's a full moon
hovering on the ridgeline of the Hawkduns
and the light's silvery-blue on the lake.

Cattle munch the river flats, sound
as if they're eating cereal, and merinos
look like blobs of cream on the Home Hills.

Milo scratches the iron walls of a hut,
scrapes dirt, whimpers and barks, smells
rats or rabbits cowering there. In

half an hour before dark I snatch six
spunky little rainbows from a ripple
on a blue and white-winged dry fly

and in homage to renewals rather than
requiems I return them all. Then we
watch the sun sink behind the Dunstans

over which the sky's an array of cerise
and gold then indigo as the dusk deepens
and moths play with the wispy breeze.

But before long we get around to
discussing one's eternal preoccupations –
where we are, and who, and what

happens to us, and how much say
we really have in all or any of that,
if prescience would only leave us alone.

FLAMENCO

In the west, imperiously, a blue door
instead of yesterday's grey and indigo clouds
that sat there sullenly all day. But now,

this evening, cerise then blood-red banners
and scarves of magenta and gold are
slowly unfolding as if the western sky

is being swept by the swirling capes of matadors.

AND

———

Here's a story. Our spirits
are fleeter than deer,
they live in the summer house
by the lake
that's jouncy in the sun.

They play in the moonlight,
a breeze like catkins
at our faces, and sing
of whatever will be,
and to hell with the past.

But we can't do that.
We're here. In the late afternoon
I stare into the sun,
not quite lost,
not quite found.

AURIPO

God made sweet little apples
    and tossed them down from the clouds
in the summertime

and their skins turned red
    and sallow yellow in the autumn
like the sky in the evenings

over the far western ranges
    before the bright bands of cirrus
made way for an orange moon

and a grand concatenation of stars

BETWEEN KOKONGA
AND KYEBURN

It's warm in the wind
and hot in the lee of trees

and the seal's shimmering.
You wander back and forth

between the stony verge
and the dotted white line

like a zipper down the middle
of the road and, as is often

the case, you're in between
where you've come from

and where you're going
and nothing's straightforward

or settled at either end.
It often looks as if la la land's

the world you live in
and every second joker

you meet or know
is kindred in that respect.

But you can thank your lucky stars
there's no virtuoso positivity guru

or bouncy life coach on hand
to give you *strategies* to help you

sort yourself out, stop being as jittery
as a bully in shallows. And yet,

maybe it's true that a man
has to have a reason

to lift above and beyond just being.
And looking dead ahead and floating

there's the Buster and Kyeburn
and the Kakanuis tending khaki

in the late summer sun, and above them
a blue sky flecked with cumulus

white as marshmallows,
all of them there because of

arrangements defying comprehension,
and none have cause to ponder

or be irked by questions to do with
to be, or not to be.

Yet again, you're aware
that living one's life

isn't as simple as crossing
an open field, and,

upon the upland road,
in the only land

you'll ever get to know much about,
your lies unravel behind you;

nonetheless, enough truths
canter alongside

to help keep you alive
for the time being.

CADENCES OF SPRING, LATE AUGUST

Light snow has fallen in flurries all day,
    the tenth fall since April,
and still winter will not cease.

The dry wood is nearly all gone
    but the sun is warmer
than for months, the shadows

less like giant capes, thrushes
    and blackbirds and wax-eyes
everywhere urgent, jittery, magpies

practising their testiness, and plovers
    nothing but the usual nark
nark nark. The cadences of spring

are felt as much as heard, and before
    long in the evenings
you'll be walking up the trail towards

the mountains where sunsets flare.

LATE WINTER SNOW

(FOR PHIL AND STEVE)

The child has never been older
than in August
snow blanketing the countryside
and we never to be younger
greet the misty morning
sunlight spraying iridescent mountains
across the lake . . .
                    the birch trees sway
like frail dancers,
strings of light merge
and the violas of night put down their bows
as feet move in search of hands to clasp
and I say
              Lead me not into harsh ministrations
of cruellest spring
or the wells of inconsolable days
but down pathways leaf-lined to summer
in the absence of fog,
ladders of rain.

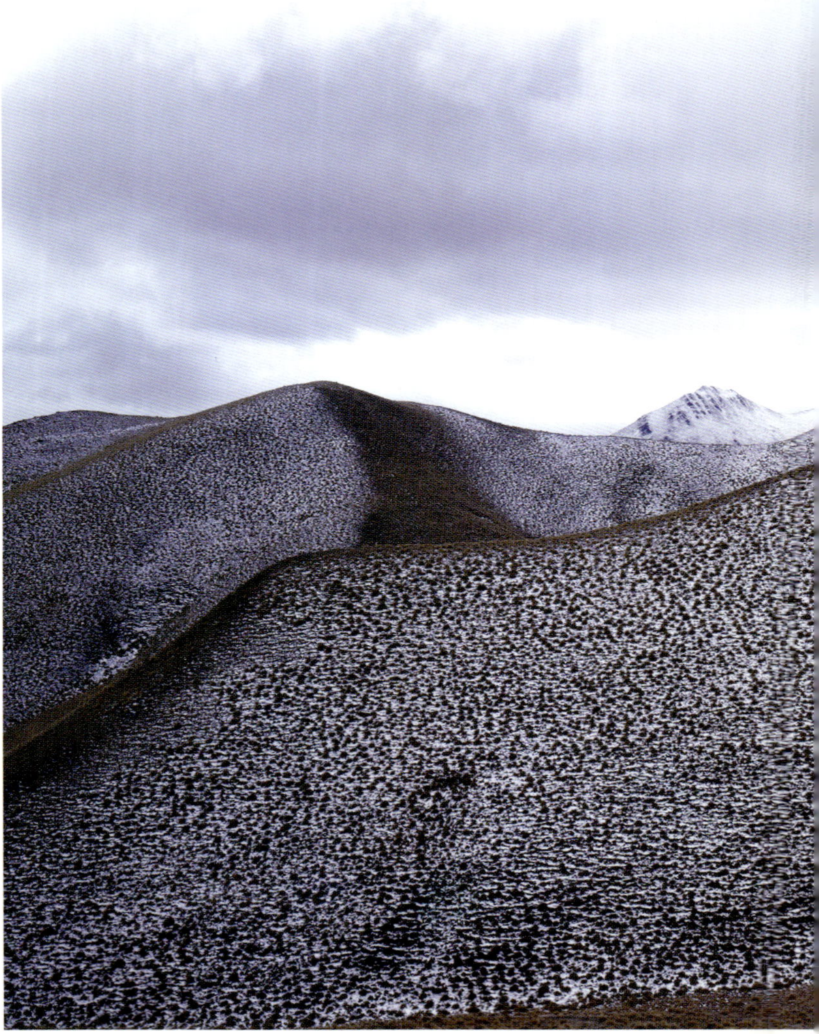

SOMEWHERE, OVER THE RAINBOW

There will be a place
in which I belong,

and there was, once
upon a time, in

sunshine and rain,
where life was more

than adornment,
on the one hand,

disillusion on the other.
There was a place;

one day you pray
you'll find it again.

HEAVEN

Don't pretend you don't want
a clump of people
to give you a tick or two
and send you on your way
glowing.

Maybe heaven is a place
in the hearts of those
who respected and honestly
liked you a lot,
an earthly place
with brightness behind you,
surreal skies above
lighting the best way home.

SNOWSTORM,
BAREWOOD PLATEAU

You find yourself telling people
    your memory's *not what it was*
and wondering if any truly
sentient human being can ever
    say they're happily unhurried,
or can be said to grow old
gracefully. It's maybe that
    dignity's hoped for as a
palliative to disappointment
or despair, drear prognoses
    in the face of those who
remark on so-and-so having had
a good innings. All right, all
    right, but you're not
thanking God for small mercies
any more, you're pleased
    to be able to go out alone
in September snow under a cold
moon and bring in wood you cut
    yourself months ago, put
it on the fire and watch it flame
stupendously; glad you're not
    like that hawk gripping
a rabbit carcass on the road
to Middlemarch this afternoon,
    snow like ash floating down,
whose last moments, feathers
flying, were a fatally defiant stare,
    and you shaken by what you'd been

unable to avoid, his compulsive
carrion convictions, your commanding
   conclusion, and what that
said about our respective places
in the pecking order of a tenuous
   ever more scouring world.

AURAS

———

The land and sky
in moon or daylight
have grace or grandeur,
sometimes both.

With us one's
not so sure,
except on grave
occasions.

BEYOND THE STARS

Almost due west
   and high in the sky
   Venus burns bright.

I've just lost another friend
   and the great star's
   sharp white light's

tinged with an aurora's
   lemony green bouncing
   off the faraway ice.

Now I'm off on another
   journey to dark places
   where one's memories

live on in the spaces
   between stars, and
   far beyond the stars.

NEAR KOKONGA

The hawk's imperious   at ease
in the glassy air   sunlight skittery
on the Taieri River   where the Kyeburn
enters   a noisy brat

If there's one message abroad
it is   Seek peace
kick revenge   lay down your arms

ON THE EDGE OF A MEADOW

The tree is complete in a cloak of green.
    I stare for hours
at the lamps of stored summer light,
                 and shiver.
    They promise too much
        when too much is incomplete.

A dead tree's branches
    are like a ladder leaning on the sky.
The breeze is a paw at my face:
        it fondles the grass
                and passes on.

And the lamps are the lights
               of happiness
    meant for when we discover
        what the world could be.

IDA VALLEY SUNSET

You go out in the evening
after a boisterous nor'west day
in the hope that the pageantry
playing out
wells long after it has faded
in the sky

and those who say
you live in the middle
of nowhere have got it wrong
unless there's nothing
welling in your head
and your heart's lost heart

SACROSANCT

A man wants to sing of the him
in where he comes from
and not sound desperately
nationalistic or vain, retain
some dignity, acknowledge
there's grace in gravity
without thunder; wants

to shake out the sombre
the way one sieves stones
from soil; to see what grows
and be able to claim, modestly,
that he had a hand in it, that
he took heart from it,
and that what grows when
we are gone sprouts, in part,
from what we were.

He yearns to recognise
what's sacrosanct.

SUMMER MORNING

A sea of cobalt blue
and the light
    beginning to shimmer
like an ocean
flecked with gold

and it's not doing,
like us, anything
    other than what
I know it's doing
to me.

END OF THE ROAD

The mountains at the end of the road
are like mountains ought to be
to one such as me, neither approachable
nor unapproachable, and requiring effort
all round. And on a good day
when the mind's in working order,
the man you used to be succours
the man you didn't want to be,
the one learning to skirt the snarls
that catch like matagouri, stab
like speargrass, slide like scree.

On river flats bare as honesty
magpies are in control, harass hawks
that harass them because it's spring,
the time when everything
comes on strong, the time when
there's no time for truncation
and none have the stamina to complain
about unsuitable regalia
on the mountains over which
the sky is a huge arena
at the end of the road.

BIRD LAND

I'm wondering what they think they're doing
   this time and if they may be making
      a big mistake – sparrows, the boys with bibs
         and the girls without, not so flaunty,

and the few remaining waxies
   with that porcelain sliver around their eyes
      and light velvety green feathers
         that I would love to stroke since they look like

smooth lustrous velour. They are all pecking
   madly at softened grains of boiled wheat
      that's squidgy and brown as day-old poo,
         and at stale bread crumbs and a bowl

of sugary water that's like stippled melting ice . . .
   they can't have seen the striped cat
      creeping through the wall-flowers
         and under the rich red japonica

and through the voluptuous red and yellow
   goblets that are splendiferous tulips. And they
      haven't; the antic pecking and squabbling
         continues until I leap from the porch

and there's a kerfuffly flurry and scatter, kapow,
   and the cat slinks away with a backward, hating
      glance at me, and I stand there in the warm sunshine
         and raise my arms and, as if I've just

scored the winning try for the All Blacks, shout,
  'I am your saviour and I love you, you perky
    little buggers, you feathered marvels, who
      put up with me and my passion for Sibelius

and Schubert and Beethoven and all the rest;
  and in my pathetic little pocket of desire to be seen
    as having a proper respect and regard for the voiceless
      and their rights to life, liberty and the pursuit

of some vestige of happiness.' And I'm urged
  to say I feel the need to share this soiled
    and stressed little planet we live on,
      and scrap over, with more than just my own

bloody-minded, apathetic, destructive, complacent
  kind, am urged to stand up like Moses
    and say, 'As you do to the least of these,
      so you do unto me . . .' until the end of our time.

CONTINUE ON

When the music stops, when what is grand
lingers only in parts of the mind
that touch the heart, a voice says *continue on*.

It's like full-blown spring, bees busy and loud
in the pink-blossomed crab apple tree, tulips
trumpeting, voluptuous, Mendelssohn's

Incidental Music from *A Midsummer Night's Dream*
defining the moment, and the bees seemingly
oblivious in blossom shimmering in the wind.

ON TOP OF THE WORLD
(FOR KILA HEPI)

The days seem longer all of a sudden
now that August's here
and inventions become realities
ingrained.

Riding between Wedderburn
and Hill's Creek we're on top
of the world, my young friend Kila
and I, the clouds like white drapery
spilling down the mountains,
and the sun's like acclamation
strobing the downs. And the angels
in their white dresses
kick their bangled heels
and dabble their feet
in the ever blue blue.

It seems that the purer
the air the greater one's ardour.
We stop and listen for the songs
of air and water and I swear
I heard the rapt sounds
of angels singing, not of Paradise lost
but Paradise now.

PRAYER IN AUTUMN

Someone somewhere will have a veil
  strong enough to deflect the lassos time swings

and leave me free to embrace integrity and candour
  without malice or pity for the carrion dishonour.

Or so I hope and pray in autumn
  when the afternoon light's blue on the mountains,

the trout are moving upstream, and the springs
  are bulging from the earth again, cool and fresh.

And I'm one of many keen to put my name down
  on the list of those wanting another spring.

SKY

—

If the sky knew half
of what we're doing
down here

it would be stricken,
inconsolable,
and we would have

nothing but rain

WITH SPRING IN MIND

When there's snow on the ground
and the sky is as clear and blue
as anywhere on earth, you write
in the springtime in your notebook,
then walk to the well
with the sound of crystals
scrunching under your boots, and
all the 'e' words – exhalation, excitement,
exhilaration, ecstasy, eternity –
arrive unbidden like a flock
of silver-eyes looking for scraps. And now
you're sure you know what's meant
by the phrase *as good as it gets*.

SUMMER AFTERNOON, ALEXANDRA

Cauliflowers float above the Old Man Range.
Fine white tresses are snagged in the sky
over the Dunstans. In Alexandra
it's 31 degrees and rising. Mums

and small children sprawl under trees
beside the museum where history's
arrested. Thirsty, burning, a few of the tots
complain, demand drinks. So far the sun's

in control. It smiles, sears, says nothing's
able to outwit me. What about
years not yet accounted for? What about
what we don't know about? What about

the big, muscled blue-black clouds
towering in the south? What about all that?

IN THE HILL'S CREEK CEMETERY

Everything says tenuous here
   where neat edging and vases of fresh flowers
are one way of trying to tidy untidy lives,

and even the empty jars
   that shine in the morning sun reflect remembrance
in all its kaleidoscopic fragmentations:

love, affection, grief . . . guilt
   about inattention when it was needed most,
apologies not made, churlishness enjoyed,

schadenfreude relished, and so on.
   What matters most can't be attended to now
in a place where guilt and sincerity

are determined to merge as self-indulgence.
   But never mind, if we're lucky the road to hell
may not be paved with good intentions

here or anywhere else where,
   in a soak close by, a heron practises dressage,
paradise ducks pretend imperious, and above us all

a hawk masters disdain. Dry grass wafts.
   Serenity's hanging on somehow despite pervasive
evidence of our mortality and, overhead, the wisps of cirrus

that tell us a big nor'wester's not far way.

EXIT

I'll go down quickly one day in autumn I hope
without fanfare   when there's a few traces only
of stringy white cloud in the great sweep of blue
I've loved so long   and the grand slumbering
high hills and burly brown ranges
will be flaunting their shadows
the ridge lines like pleats diving to the valleys

There'll be a hawk circling in slow-motion
a falcon arrowing   plovers and magpies
niggly in paddocks   mallards idling on ponds
and far above geese spearing north

The sun will be strong and bright   the grasses
bleached pale yellow and tinged with red
and the river a vivacious blue-green
where it spurts from the gorge

And friends who've stuck with me
will gather by the river
and listen to the eddying past
and my son will have come home not long before
to tell me not to fret anymore
to slow down
and to affirm how much we enjoyed
our times together

And I'll have burnt the notes I made
saying how sad I was to have found
I liked some friends more than they liked me
years ago   and that I wished
I'd found it easier to live with the mistakes
I made   and not to have been stripped bare
by the mismanagement of my personal life
and the way in which it was highlighted
by the circumstances of others

Say I was a lover
of the wide-open spaces   of empty lands
that aren't empty   of silence
that isn't silent

Say I meant well most of the time

DESIRE

To do what most hardly ever
or never dream of

before we all
go to the same dark

and private place,
joys winnowed

and all the what ifs
and might have beens

carried off as ash
on the wind,

one's only memorials
worth a candle

the fading recollections
of those

who truly loved us
before we left.

PART THREE

WATER

RIVER WIND

The wind may let us down
but it never fails. The wind
carries dark clouds
on its shoulders
and totters down
from the mountains.

And there comes a time
when all hills
are mountains. Now is the time.
If rain is to fall
let it fall gently
on the shoulders of the mountains,
and let it run quietly
and quickly
into the river
that feels the light in the sky
and prizes the light.

Instinctively
you know what the river is saying
without being told. You hear
what the river is singing
without knowing the words
to the song. You know where
the river is going
and that it doesn't know
what you know, that it tempts you
to envy
and the feeling returns, and returns.

TAIERI RIVER, PAERAU

The hills, in mist or in the dire heat of day
    aren't lacquered in sweat as the oxbows are,
as the river is where it meanders across the peneplain
        and the downiest of cumulus clouds
are reflected there where the water idles and eddies.

There's time to wile and wiliness drifts into the reeds
    and cress, and spectres resembling peace of mind
appear on the skyline across the valley, call to you
        by name, invite you to look to the heavens
and ponder what's visible in the fabulous sky.

THE ANGLER

Thinking, All love is curious,
    and, Discord becomes impossible
  in time, I concentrate on the simple,
rhythmic task in hand,
    cast a fly upstream

and watch it jog towards me
    on the water tumbling
  and shambling along. I potter
as anglers do, dawdle, wander slowly
    upriver, working my cares out

as I work the kinks from the line
    on every cast. The sun throbs,
  the earth throbs, and all round me
the mountains take their used to time.
    And the river, which

never gives tongue to contrition
    in a language to which
  we subscribe, runs clear
beneath a no best-used-by blue sky.
    The sun swings

as the line swings down and across
    the pool. The breeze
  talks of Once upon a time. The river
is Life in mime. If I were to rid myself
    of this whipping rod

and ride the rolling river down . . .
    but I don't, instead
  I gather the line again and make
another, similar, careful cast:
    and the wind speaks

of Once upon a cowardly time
    yet another pawky time,
  and the Orphean sun bids the stones
dance and sing of all there is to cherish
    if one takes the time.

DECLARATION

The bed of the river's
    like a ransacked room
and the banks are cloaked
    with lime-green willows
that toss and flail
    in a summer gale

and you're convinced
    that only what's sacred
and isn't wounded
    stands between us
and oblivion, and
    without reverence

for the world we inhabit
    we will never come
to cherish the planet
    we depend on
and have yet to learn
    how to love and protect

for as long
    as we all shall live.

AUDIBLE

The creek is in trouble,
troubled, its trickle
close to vanishing
in a bed of gravel.

A wish to be audible
is a fight for life.
In that sense
there's little difference
between us.

SUMMER SONG

The wind sings
anywhere and
everywhere,

and so does
the river
for as long as
there's rain.

DROUGHTBREAKER

After months without rain,
prayer and meditation
exhausted, I saw the farmer

standing at the window,
tears on his face
streaming like moonlight.

WEATHERING

———————————————

Fog for days, ice like
pendants on the trees,
frost jewelling the ground,
the sun trying hard

to break through. Grit
sparkles on the road,
the fire crackles and spits.
Your lungs don't like this,

and joints click. What
choice but to weather
the weathering until you
hear the water start

to trickle, the first lumps
of ice break on the earth.

HIGH COUNTRY RIVER

The river holds every note for as long
as we care to listen. It works its way
down country, swings and swerves,
surges, bounds and starts to say
I'm hurrying, I'm hurrying, then kicks
up its heels and sparks fly as it gallops
along for a bit, slows and glides sedately
down a long pool; and clouds' smeary
reflections are as if gouache is more
than a medium suggesting movement
stilled, and yet the river bounds on
uninhibited to the grinding
graunch and rumble of boulders
and the musketry-clatter of shining stones.

GREY LAKE

Things happen unexpectedly in the hills,
    under stippled and rivuleted pale cliffs
        from which pigeons coo and rabbits

peer from beady burrows, and above which
    hawks patrol, drift slowly back and forth,
        relaxed yet surveillant. Nothing

stops us in our tracks more than anxiety,
    and spasming reactions to what one hears
        and sees; and then, what one feels returns

as what one comes to know.
    From that essentials flow.

ANCESTORS

(FOR PHIL TEMPLE)

I came this way to shed some care.
Every stone I stumbled on, every

root that snagged my foot was
bastard discontent. By the time

I'd reached the hut I was too tired
to complain anymore. Shucking my pack

I lay in the grass that shimmered
in the breeze. The blue sky

preened itself. Wheels of sunlight
bowled along the valley. I dozed off

until evening crept over forest
and mountain. I knew they would

find me sometime. My speechless ancestors
played like mice among my dreams.

It grew cold. And colder. I woke
to the river running over my bed

of stone. I have come to know
that where a river sings a river

always sang. I listen.
This much I have learned.

SLIDING BY

The river's not so solitary
the way you're turning out to be

and maybe it's better at life.
You've been walking

down by the river, you've
been talking to the wide river,

you've been observing
the rivers of sky in the river

running by, and bye and bye
is what time says to you

and the river sliding by
sly as sly. And when you

step in the river and go
to cross to the other side

you pause half way
and the water piles high

against your thigh
as you wonder whether

to go forward or back,
where you've been, what you had.

SOURCES

When you look at the sky in the river
and the rivers in the sky
the clouds are currents streaming by
without a hesitant word of a lie.

On the spur of more than the moment
you lay down, shut your eyes
and listened to the source of all rivers
above and below flowing by.

And you lay there thinking
about what was the right thing to do
in the circumstances and if such
is, therefore, a good thing to do.

But all you could see were clouds
in the sky, and all you could hear
was the river running by. Neither
of them known to tell you a lie.

TAIERI DAYS

How far off those days, never mine
and never not mine, when
the only poems I knew
were the bursting greens of willows
by the Taieri in spring,
greens of cress and water weed
and the grass that sheep grazed
incognito because they all
looked much the same.

But the sky never did,
the clouds never did
shaped like tubes, plates, slats,
piles of rubble, knucklebones
and bunting streaming before the stars.

The river sprang and shone,
had a shifty and open
arrangement with skies
arcing and stretching
over the Maungatua
and Rock and Pillar ranges.

I didn't want to own
or sell anything so grand
and communal as land;
all I needed
was the right to belong,
one's spirit all the colours
of the spectrum,
like the sky.

SOMEWHERE, A RIVER

Always you can hear a river
somewhere singing

like a wind in trees
or in the loftiest stretch

of cirrus heading east
with an exotic flourish

at the end of days
when you started out

heavy and finished up
light, days that showed

how easy it was to move
from A to B when A

is for anxiety and B
for the brilliance

which opens the doors
to clarity before completion.

Always, somewhere,
there's a river, singing.

ELEGY IN THE CLUTHA VALLEY
(IN MEMORY OF DENIS GLOVER)

Something we will never know
the reason for
or the answer to
woke me one January morning
and streamed through the half-open window
and made me feel it was timeless,

and I remembered a day
that will always be long ago
when I was older
and better able
to stride off over the rolling downs
in search of all the best reasons

in the beleaguered world
to do or not to do,
and to be in touch with oneself
wherever heart and mind
had come to agree
on where we should be going,

and let us think this
could be so. Then, the world's ill
flew from the shoulder
of the highest hill
around, and thereafter the will
took a bolder part in things

and my heart leapt
to the blind mountain
from which scree flaked
and water bled all day long
to the downy valley floor
where, in the evening

I took my rod and my heart
to the river's side
and cast and cast
while water
ran purple and gold
in the quickening dusk,

and the sedges
fleeing the river
were like ash
at my face and throat
and all the world
seemed to be timeless.

FROM AFAR

A friend asks what I miss most,
aside from friends and foes,
and I say, Most is hard to answer,
but try this: the saurian backs
of high country lands; real rivers
and mountains; ice and snow
and winds that know how to blow;
high, crusty white clouds by day
and orange and red and gold
and green lenticulars above the ranges
in the evenings. And even more
the sounds of brisk running water
and the clear, hard, sharp light
in the grandest blue skies of all.

EARLY SUMMER

Down by the lake,
under craggy rocks,
I stood and looked
at confusions of stars,
at the yoke-coloured moon.

A light breeze furred
my cheeks, and not far
off, in the gorge, I heard
the clink of oars
in rowlocks, and wondered

if Charon was on his way
and won't be wanting
to hear what my heart
tells me to say.

BELLS ACROSS THE MEADOWS

I walk by the river
   which talks in my sleep,
reflects clouds cruising
  in seas of blue,
and mutes the sounds
   of winds in the willows
and alpine grasslands.
  And someone, a musician
and painter and a whole lot
   else, says he believes
when we die we go into
   'an ocean of love and mercy'.

But that's not what I would
  choose, given the chance:
and now that I am almost old,
   give me love, mercy and
the courage to extend them,
  and have them accepted with
gratitude before I go into the ether
   listening to the ringing
of bells across the meadows.

THE RIVER IN YOU

(AFTER W S MERWIN)

―――――――――

The first thing you want to hear
is the river sound

and then to see
the source of that sound

for it's never the same
yet it's always something like

what you think you remember
from the time before

and the one before that
and when you reach the bank

though you no longer hurry
as you used to and look down

on the long reach that flows south
and curves east like a wing

light and sound are one
and you know the swirl

of having been there before
though it's not quite the same

as last time and the time
before that and you sense the pull

that draws you back is the river in you
racing to keep time with the river sound

PART FOUR

AIR

——

TAKING OFF

I take off for the hills
where gulls circle
and soar in the thermals
as if caught
in the sky's blue plughole
when in fact
their flight's elan
where the nor'wester
flips off the ridges
and the tussock's
restless and shines
on the hillsides,
inland Otago's
vast acres
browning in the sun.

I take off for the hills
to escape the rage
of my neighbour's mower
savaging grass,
to find some breathing space,
and find the wonder is
wonder hasn't died,
happiness beckons,
and the wind in the tussock murmurs
And not before time.

WINGS OF THE WIND

The big wind's birthplaces
are south and west of here
in gales that rant and rave
and buffet, that jostle and bully
and berate, a wild magnificence
of might without spite.

Breezes come from elsewhere,
parts benign, gentler,
bringing respite that leads
to ease. They fluff, sigh,
tickle. What comes gently,
slowly drifting in, leaves

without rancour, or haste.
If you don't love
and applaud that, luxuriate
there, you're still searching
for what blows in best
on the wings of the wind.

CYCLING IN THE MANIOTOTO

I wouldn't care to hear
why it's said we're here
in case it ruins
what it feels like now.

The meaning of life
being played out
on the undulations between
Ranfurly and Kyeburn

on a bristly summer's day
is not part of the
metaphysical agenda
as far as I know.

There's no need to worship
the God of all gracious things:
the only one worth
honouring is the will

to keep on resolutely
keeping on. I baa at sheep,
shout at magpies, moo
with cattle, marvel at

the panache of hawks
riding the air above
the Ida Range. And I ride,
my legs going round

faster than in months,
the sou'easter a helpful
lick and flutter, and
past Wedderburn,

on the gentle incline
down the straights
to Oturehua, in the distance
the skyline of the Old Man Range

is a high wire
on which the last
of the snow is caught
like strands of wool.

FLIGHT

On the slow wing-beat
of a curious falcon
my wishes belonged.
I rose and spiralled
on thermals
and the mountains smiled
all afternoon.

The falcon's wings
splintered the autumn sunlight
above the remnant fog
that sat on the river
like a marquee
and water scrawled inscriptions
on every stone.

ONCE

———

upon a time
the earth
was happy enough
without us.

Such a time
may come again,
and little
but insects
and grass
will rock
to the rueful sounds
of the wind.

FLYING SOUTH

Your fonder memories
are the shiny haloes
propellors make
on flights
over mountains
on clear days
when you're
on your way home.

FIRST DAY OF SPRING

The clouds are more black than white
  in the blue today
from all that grappling and battering
      when scaling the ranges

in the north and west. Cumulus, mainly,
  they bustle over us, making
for the burred ocean in the east. It's true
      what I'm telling you you'd see

if you were here with me, enjoying
  September's sun while eating
an orange, stroking a stray grey cat,
      and reading about Henri Cartier-Bresson,

recently dead, who said 'There is only
  the present, the present and eternity.'

Air

195

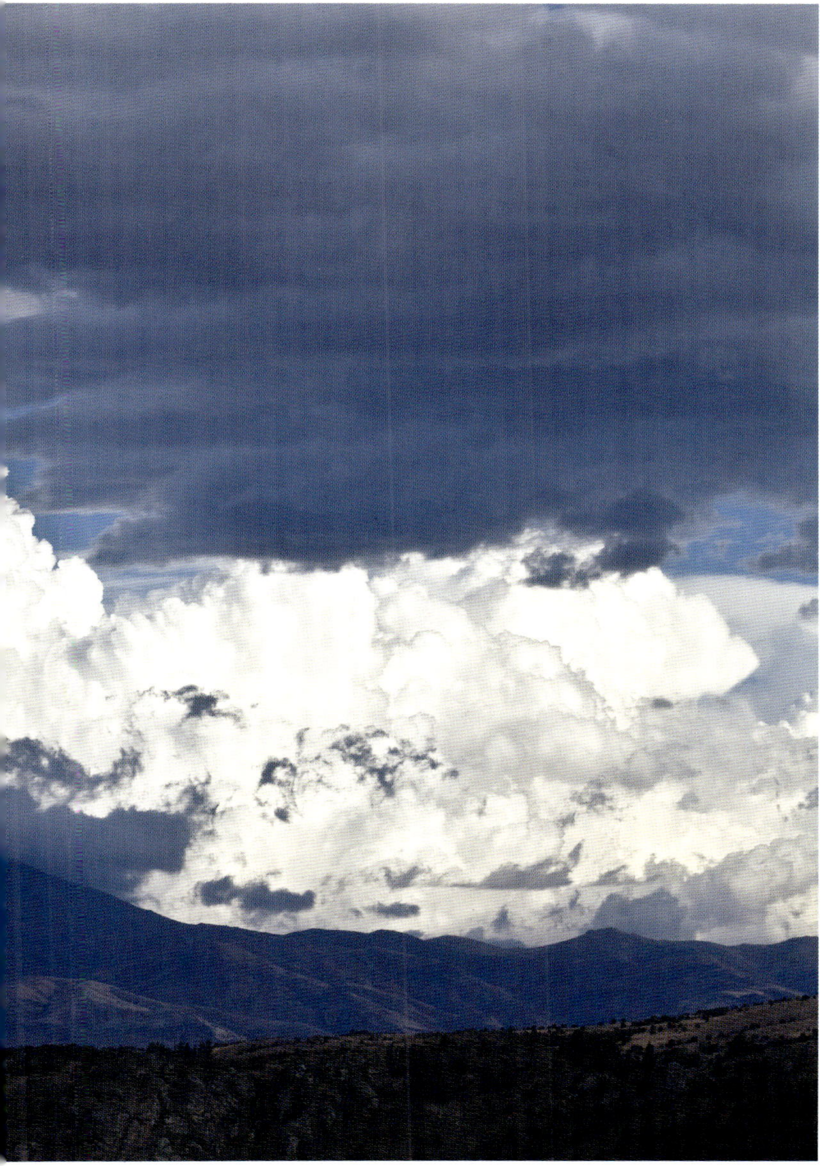

HAWKDUN SUMMER

In the dun valleys
the wind's your life talking
morning, noon, and evening
before fields of stars
cluster above the pleated Hawkduns
and you're left feeling
either less, or more, harried,
because that's fate
when you're in between.

And there are days when
a breeze ruffles the valley's grasses
and the Ida's a broad shallow sound,
and there are times
when time alone passes
and a temperament you can't deny
accentuates the view
of unquenchable blue. And that's
when you're most
like you.

HAWKS IN A GALE

Hawks pendulum in the gale.
They're looking for field mice,
young rabbits, birds, anything
dead or alive, and their flight's
panic-punctuated grace
fine tuning their desperation.

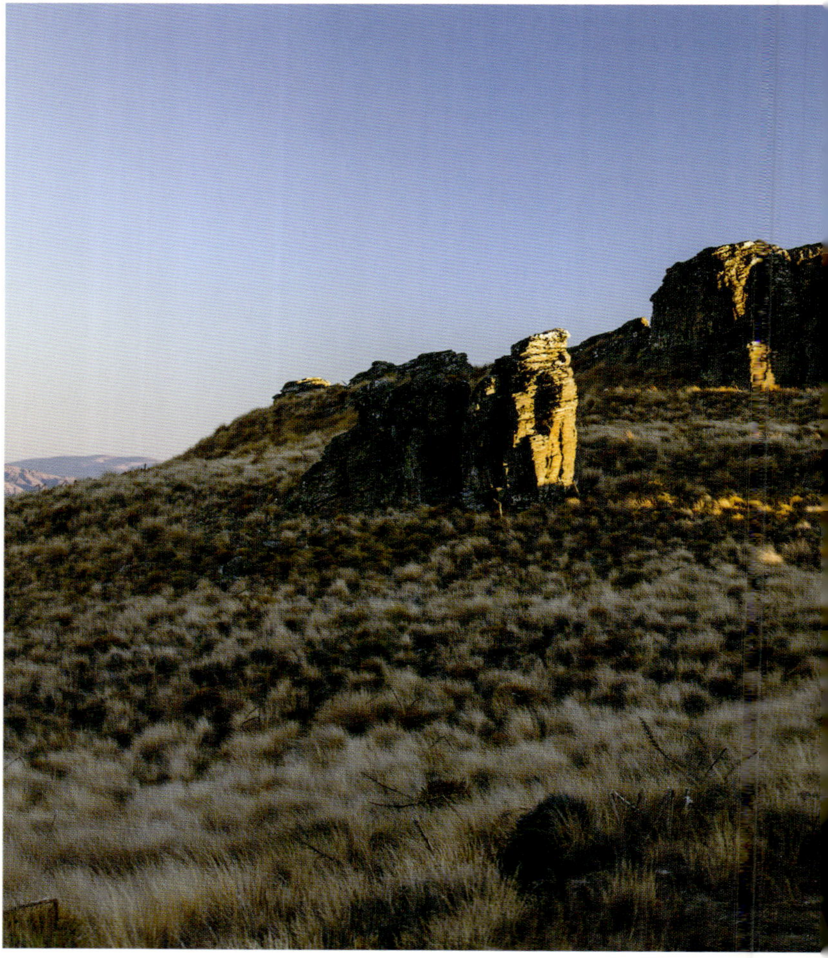

SPRING NOR'WESTER

The nor'wester gallops over and
down from the mountains,
races over the downlands, canters
in the lee of a wind-break,
cusses in a dry-grassed gulley.

On days like this magpies
are more irascible, plovers
irked instead of disdainful,
oystercatchers more crotchety,
herons sheltering wisps, hawks

peeved yet still persistent, relentless.
Today, buffet and restless
mean much the same, except
to sheep and cattle who confirm
it's four legs good, two less so.

There's no trick, no marvel, no gift
behind the art of standing stalwart,
staunch and upright here, just
the chance that blind nature gives,
then takes away. And don't we know it.

FORETOLD

(FOR L NCHT AND HELEN)

There's a warm breeze blowing down
off the mountains
now that most of the snow has gone.

There's a song somewhere
in the hearts of every man and woman
with the heart to sing.

There's elation born of relief
and the return of hope and grace
in the flight of a hawk over Rough Ridge.

There's beauty in the unruffled
olive green and grey feathers of silver-eyes
feeding on sugar on my schist stone wall.

There's rivers and streams that are
quieter again, and sheep and cattle
whose stoicism never falters.

There's the feeling exile's over,
and that, for all its limitations,
what's foretold has barely begun.

JUST POSSIBLY

If the harrier hawk
on a fencepost
beside the highway
to Poolburn
knew disdain
you'd say
she practised it,
and imperiousness,
an ability to see
in ways we don't.

We're ghosts, say
physicists, and yet
most of what is said,
what we're told,
what we discern,
is untrue. Never-
theless, it may be
that whatever
one sees
in the sky, on

the face of the moon,
and in the winking
of the stars,
may give us
wings, talons,
and a beadier eye
with which
to better
scrutinise
this world.

MARCH RIDE

There are peaks in the sky
above the peaks in the north and west,
St Bathans lording it, the Hawkduns
scuffed yet seemly as always.

The wind and sun and rain
shapes them all. At the Moa Creek corner
I turn into the wind
and set off for home, watch

herons flung sideways
like blue-grey rags, see ardent shivers
skelter across a silvered pond
and listen for cadence

in lulls between gusts in the gale
that's lifting soil off ploughed paddocks
and sending it south
in plumes like smoke.

DARWINIAN

You can understand why Darwin
    spent much of his life

trying to learn all he could
    about the origin of species –

observing, delving, musing – but
    the jury's still out

on how much that tells us
    about why we do what we do

in the name of aspiration, vengeance,
    honour and justice, wherever

that dares to prevail, and whatever
    holds up in the name of love.

BUTTERFLIES

Some of the prettier pieces
torn from the tapestry of paradise

they flutter, palpitate and preen,
their bright cloth caught

in webs of sunshine
until they're flung up and away

and it's farewell as they ride
wild nor'westerly waves of air.

NOR'WEST ARCH

A day for dinner sets
crockery and casseroles
in northwestern skies

the arch a grand proscenium
with mountains like curtains
fallen to the floor

ON THE SLOPES OF
THE DUNSTANS

Frost's 'sweetest dream
that nature knows'
is not disclosed, is
only ever hinted at
until a dream of yours
is apprehended
unexpectedly.
        And then,
no longer a dream
a swathe of golden light
unfolds on the land,
starlight in waves
hurries across the pond,
and the sky's
a giant wheel
laced with spokes
flashing like knives
of the sun.
        It's January
and the winds of summer
unravel skeins of cloud
all the way from Mt Ida
to the Kakanuis.

WIND

You hear the wind
before you feel it,
see it harassing
defenceless leaves
and listen to limbs creak.

The rowan's suddenly a mass
of nervy red light, the agapanthus
plots of antic asterisks,
the tulips swaying back and forth
like worshippers about to speak

in tongues. The wind's a ferret
angry in the grass,
a cuff on the ear,
an irritant tousling one's hair.

WHAT THE WIND KNOWS

I don't know
  what the wind
knows of me

    but I would
love to know
  what the wind

knows
    that I don't
know

AUTUMN NOR'WESTER

There's a sea of turbulence in the trees,
    needles in the air like bran.
The long grass is being flayed
           except where it cowers
in the lee of a hedge.

Sheets of iron flap on the hay shed
    where a few nails pop like thorns.
'She's a good one,' my mate says,
        'hang on to your undies.'

THE GREAT WHERE ARE WE

When gods were young
This wind was old.
                    — Edward Thomas

Find a hollow like a flue
on the hillside
and sprawl and watch
the dramas unfold
in the great where are we,
the sky.

Then listen to the wind
that's older
than Methuselah,
singing the songs
earth intuits in us.

THE WAY IS IS

That you love nature is easy to say
until you learn that unless you act accordingly
it will call you to account in the end.

                              That's why
we're required to make the connection
between the sound the wind makes
when it starts the leaves quivering
and the way the white canes of sunlight
line the spaces between the trees
on a summer's morning.

                         It's a case
of working out what's here
for the long haul
and if we want to be part of it.
It's marvellous, abominable, confusing,
exultant: the way things are,
the way is is.

ST BATHANS IN SUMMER

The wind has dropped
so the sun is going west
any time now. There's
yellow, gold, red
and mauve in the sky,

and on the shoulders
of hills like offcuts
fallen from the clouds.
And somewhere unique
in our experience,

in a far gulley, perhaps,
and at the centre
of heart's desire, there is
peace and quiet, a
tranquil, blessed calm.

IDA VALLEY, JANUARY

This is the time
  when the windows
    rattle in the nor'wester,
      scotch thistles prepare to seed
    and the lucerne's waving acres
  of violet and green. Young thrushes
and blackbirds risk their lives
  on the ground. My neighbour's cat,
    gingery, austere, is meant
      to protect the raspberries
    from the avians and doesn't.
  I go to bed only half-pie
sound in mind and body
  and the mind starts roving,
    wars with sleep, always
      finds something else
to take issue with.

HIGH SUMMER ABOVE
THE LOGANBURN
(FOR GRAHAME)

On the Old Dunstan Road
across the Lammermoor

tussock shines and shakes,
the land an ancient

slumbering beast
whose coat's ruffling

in the wind, and over
the blue of the lake

a few knobbly cumulus
float between awed

and inconspicuous us
and a blue lake of sky.

LAKESIDE

A sharp, puffy southerly
blows up the lake
so I sit in the sunny
front seat of my car
and watch a small yacht
heel, periodically
wave surrender.

At the roadside edge
of the gravel beach
birds chitter and sing
in a scraggy tree, peck
the last, reddest wild apples
of the season.

It may be autumn
but today it feels
like spring to me.

AUTUMN SONG
(FOR SHONA AND MICHAEL)

On the road again to somewhere west,
   the morning sun's badgering the fog
cloaking the Poolburn, and over the hill
in Ophir where evening primrose
   and tall holly hocks sway by the roadside.

Further on, past the Tiger Hills, grey-white
   and black donkeys graze under turning willows
beside the Chatto Creek Hotel. I've both
expectation and a wistful melancholy swirl
   in my heart which comes and goes.

It's as if one's rooted to the spot as well
   as moving through the countryside
safe in the knowledge that my friends
share similar moments in time
   for the time being, wherever they are,

and there is still time before time
   is stilled. And on the way back gossamers
of high white cloud stream above the Ida
where lambs are half-buried and busy
   in the last of the lucerne

while mobs of ewes lie like maggots
    beside glassy ponds, sedated by the sun.
To the northwest the long line of the Dunstans
are a buff brown, Mt St Bathans blue-tinted,
    and the crinkled Hawkduns bar

the way at the head of the valley. White
    butterflies dither in off-white yarrow
and alight among the last of the mauve clover.
There's a softening of the light as the sun slides
    further and further west and I drive

slowly up the valley towards Oturehua
    dreaming of love and peace, listening
to Domingo singing Bach's *Ave Maria*
and Franck's *Panis Angelicus*, and I think
    at last I know what is true, what wonder is.

ACKNOWLEDGEMENTS

A cknowledgements for the foreword are as follows: Wendell Berry, *The Unforeseen Wilderness* (Shoemaker & Hoard, 2006); Aldo Leopold, *A Sand County Almanac* (Oxford University Press, 1949); Brian Turner, *Into the Wider World* (Random House, 2008); Brian Turner, *Somebodies and Nobodies* (Random House, 2002); Robert Macfarlane, *The Guardian* (July 2005); Bill McKibben, *Wandering Home* (Crown Publishers, New York, 2005); Margaret Atwood, *New York Review of Books* (8 April 2010); Dave Witherow and Alan Mark, 'Place: Reflections by Twelve Otago Identities', *Portrait Busts* by Louisa Baillie (Frayed Frisket Press, 2012).

T he poems 'Late Winter Snow' and 'Pastoral' were published in the volume *Ladders of Rain* (John McIndoe, 1978); 'Ancestors' in *Ancestors* (John McIndoe, 1981); 'Elegy in the Clutha Valley' in *Listening to the River* (John McIndoe, 1983); 'Lawrence Cemetery', 'On the Edge of a Meadow' in *Bones* (John McIndoe, 1985); 'Abandoned Homestead', 'Alp', 'Flight',

'Place', 'River Wind', 'Tangata Whenua' in *All that Blue Can Be* (John McIndoe, 1989); 'And', 'Van Morrison in Central Otago' in *Beyond* (John McIndoe, 1992); 'Dogs', 'Remembering Summer', 'Taking Off', 'The Angler', 'The River in You', 'Through', 'Yellow Flowers, Oturehua' in *Taking Off* (Victoria University Press, 2001); 'Beasts', 'Close of Day, Oturehua', 'Cycling in the Maniototo', 'End of the Road', 'Exit', 'Flying South', 'Heaven', 'On Top of the World', 'On the Slopes of the Dunstans', 'Poolburn Twilight', 'Sacrosanct', 'Sliding By', 'The Way Is Is' in *Footfall* (Random House, 2005); 'Hawks in a Gale', 'Hills', 'Home Hills, February', 'Ida Valley, January', 'March Ride', 'The Great Where Are We' in *The Six Pack* (New Zealand Book Month with Whitireia Publishing, 2006); 'Deserts, for Instance', 'Foretold', 'In the Hill's Creek Cemetery', 'Last Outing', 'Moving Stock', 'Sky', 'What It's Like', 'Wind' in *Just This* (Victoria University Press, 2009); 'Audible', 'Autumn Song', 'Bird Land', 'Continue On', 'Filming at Lower Nevis', 'Lakeside', 'Snowstorm, Barewood Plateau' and 'What the Wind Knows' (as 'Wind') in *Inside Outside* (Victoria University Press, 2011); 'Near Kokonga' and 'Prayer in Autumn' in *Into the Wider World* (Random House, 2008).

'Biking the Central Otago Rail Trail' and 'Taieri Days' appeared in *Quadrant*.

'Music in the Mountains' and 'Nor'west Arch' appeared in the *New Zealand Alpine Journal*.

'Looking for Real Life and the Real World' and 'West Over the Maniototo' appeared in *Landfall*.

The following poems have not been published before: 'Apple Picking', 'Applications', 'Auras', 'Auripo', 'Autumn Nor'wester', 'Bells Across the Meadows', 'Between Kokonga and Kyeburn', 'Beyond the Stars', 'Bracken', 'Butterflies', 'Cadences of Spring, Late August', 'Darwinian', 'Desire', 'Declaration', 'Droughtbreaker', 'Early Summer', 'Ensemble', 'Falls Dam', 'Farmer', 'First Day of Spring', 'Flamenco', 'From Afar', 'Grey Lake', 'Hawkdun Summer', 'High Country River', 'High Summer Above the Loganburn', 'Homecoming', 'Ida Valley Sunset', 'July, Maniototo', 'Just Possibly', 'Keep it Up', 'Matakanui', 'Once', 'Once Green', 'Opportunity Knocks', 'Rock and Pillar', 'Ruminations in the Maniototo', 'Somewhere, a river', 'Somewhere, over the rainbow', 'Sources', 'Spring Nor'wester', 'St Bathans in Summer', 'Summer Afternoon, Alexandra', 'Summer Morning', 'Summer Song', 'Taieri River, Paerau', 'There You Are', 'Weathering', 'Wings of the Wind', 'With Spring in Mind'.

Many people have helped with and encouraged me to publish a substantial collection of poems related to my liking for Central Otago. In particular I would like to thank Barbara Larson, Michael Harlow, Shona Neehoff, Philip Temple, Grahame Sydney and Gilbert van Reenen for their support in this regard.

IMAGE LOCATIONS

INDEX OF POEMS

H

I

J

K

L

M

ABOUT THE POET

One of New Zealand's finest poets and prose writers,
Brian Turner's many books include numerous volumes of
poetry, the fine memoir *Somebodies and Nobodies* and the
'miscellany' *Into the Wider World*. He was the Te Mata Poet
Laureate from 2003–2005 and was awarded an Honorary
Doctorate by the University of Otago in 2011. He is an
ardent and accomplished sportsman, conservationist and
champion of our wild places. Brian lives in Oturehua in
the Ida Valley, Central Otago.

ABOUT THE PHOTOGRAPHER

Photographic artist Gilbert van Reenen has lived
and worked in Central Otago for 35 years, initially as
a veterinarian and more recently as a professional
photographer and publisher. He is a regional trustee for
Te Araroa, New Zealand's long walking trail, and has
served three terms on the Otago Conservation Board.
He has published three books of his distinctive images
of the country's southern regions and has contributed
to several others. He has previously collaborated with
Brian Turner on exhibitions matching Brian's poems
to his images. Gilbert lives near Wanaka with his wife,
Robyn, who is a fabric artist.